W9-DDA-713

WITHDRAWN

WRITE NOW™
A Kid's Guide to Nonfiction Writing

Writing to
INSTRUCT

Jill Jarnow

The Rosen Publishing Group's
PowerKids Press™
New York

Published in 2006 by The Rosen Publishing Group, Inc.
29 East 21st Street, New York, NY 10010

Copyright © 2006 by The Rosen Publishing Group, Inc.

First Edition

Editor: Frances E. Ruffin
Book Design: Emily Muschinske

Photo Credits: Cover and p. 1 (girls) © Ed Bock/CORBIS;
cover and p. 1 (boy) © Tom & Dee Ann McCarthy/CORBIS;
p. 9 © Roy Morsch/CORBIS; p. 15 © Adriana Skura; p. 17
© Photodisc; p. 21 © Mike Donnellan.

Library of Congress Cataloging-in-Publication Data

Jarnow, Jill.
Writing to instruct / Jill Jarnow.— 1st ed.
     v. cm. — (Write now : a kid's guide to nonfiction writing)
Includes bibliographical references and index.
Contents: Writing to instruct — Giving instructions is a skill —Organizing
your instructions — Writing how-to instructions — Using graphs
to instruct — Science experiments — Instructions for a recipe —
Using maps as resources — Writing a speech that instructs —
Helpful words that instruct.
ISBN 1-4042-2834-9 (lib. bdg.) — ISBN 1-4042-5321-1 (pbk.)
1. English language—Composition and exercises—Study and teaching
(Early childhood)—Juvenile literature. 2. Exposition (Rhetoric)—
Juvenile literature. 3. Language arts (Early childhood)—Juvenile
literature. [1. English language—Composition and exercises.] I. Title.
LB1139.5.L35J353 2005
372.62'3—dc22
                                                      2003024454

Manufactured in the United States of America

Contents

Writing to Instruct

Has anyone ever given you directions for getting somewhere that were too hard to follow? Have you ever tried to put together a toy from **instructions** that were hard to understand? We follow instructions almost every day of our lives. You listen to your teacher's instructions to take a test. Drivers follow road signs that **instruct** them to take new routes to avoid storms or bad road conditions. Workers follow their employers' instructions to make a product or to provide a service. In this book you will learn how to write different kinds of instructions that are clear and easy to read.

A Scavenger Hunt

A scavenger hunt is a kind of treasure hunt. Players are given a list of items to find within a period of time. The players are also supplied with a map. The person who finds the most objects in the time period is the winner. Here is an example of a scavenger hunt.

INSTRUCTIONS:

Here is a map of the Mulberry neighborhood. Look for the items on your list. You have 15 minutes to check off each item and to show where you found it on the map.

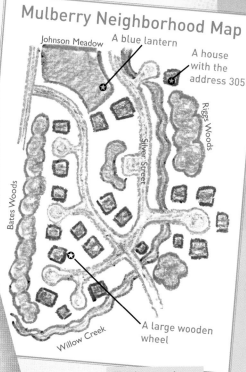

Mulberry Neighborhood Map

Johnson Meadow

A blue lantern

A house with the address 305

Riggs Woods

Silver Street

Bates Woods

A large wooden wheel

Willow Creek

Scavenger Hunt List

- A blue lantern ✓
- A large wooden wheel ✓
- A tree with red ribbons
- A striped wind sock
- A mailbox shaped like a barn
- A house with the address 305 ✓
- A stuffed owl in a window
- A sign with a large yellow arrow

The instructions tell the reader what he or she has to do and how much time there is to do it.

Giving Instructions Is a Skill

Being able to write easy-to-follow instructions is a skill that takes organized thinking and practice. Make a list of your **information** so that you can put it in the right order. It is a good idea to make a numbered list of steps or **materials** that will be described in your instructions. Add **details** that will be helpful. For example, to tell a friend how to find your house, give your house number and the name of the street and mention nearby side streets. Explain which buses or subways to take there. Describe the color of your house and any special features it has, such as a porch swing or trees in the front yard.

A Note from Stacy

Numbered steps make instructions easy to follow.

Dear Jo;

Here is how to get to our new house.

1. We live at 244 Broad Street.

2. Take the Broad Street bus and get off at Green Avenue and Broad Street.

3. Our house is four doors down from Green Avenue, on the left side.

4. Our house is yellow and it has a white playhouse in the side yard. I will be looking out of my window for you.

Your Friend,

Stacy

Note any features that will help to make your house easier to find.

Organizing Your Instructions

To write clear, understandable instructions, you must be familiar with what you are describing. Picture yourself reading and using the instructions that you are going to write. Write an **introductory paragraph** that tells your reader what he or she needs to know. Read what you have written. Are your instructions in order? If not, number each step and arrange them in the correct order. Did you forget any steps? Include details that can help the reader to follow your instructions. However, do not confuse the reader with too much information. If you have written unimportant details, take them out.

How to Feed My Cat

Dear Chris,

I will be away at my grandmother's house this weekend. I am glad that you can feed my cat, Rusty. His bowls are on the floor in the kitchen. Please scrape the old leftover food into the garbage under the sink. Then wash the bowl. Open the can of cat food (it has a pop-top lid) that I left on the counter. Empty the food into the bowl. Put the bowl back on the floor for Rusty to reach. Rinse out his water bowl and fill it with fresh water. Please feed him in the morning on Saturday, October 9, and Sunday, October 10. If you have time, please pat Rusty for a few minutes after he has finished eating. I know that he will be lonely with everybody away. My dad is driving us to my grandmother's in his new car. If you need to reach me, I will be at (663) 555-9876.

Thank You,

Peter

Start your paragraph by telling the reader what he or she needs to do.

Move the sentence about times to feed Rusty to the beginning of the note.

Leave out unimportant details!

9

Writing How-to Instructions

Write Right!

To write instructions on building or assembling something, draw a simple picture to help the reader understand.

Someday you may have to write a set of instructions to create or **assemble** something, such as a toy or a piece of **equipment**. As discussed in earlier chapters, make sure that you put the steps in your instructions in order. Include a list of the materials, tools, and equipment that the reader should have on hand. If it is a project that might be hard to do, be sure to include helpful hints on what to do. Finally, either type the instructions or be sure that your writing is neat.

How to Make a Safety-Nose Airplane

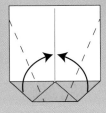

Materials:
- ☐ 8¹/₂- by-11-inch (21.6-by-27.9 cm) sheet of paper

What you need to do:
- ☐ Work on a clean, flat desk or table.

List any materials that the reader will need to follow your instructions.

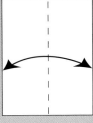

1. Fold the paper in half lengthwise, or the long way. Then unfold. This makes a crease, or a deep fold, down the center of the paper.

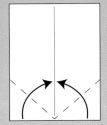

2. Fold the bottom corners of the paper so that they line up with the center crease line. The bottom edge of the plane should look like a triangle.

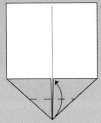

3. Fold the sharp point of the plane in half, crosswise. Folding the point makes the nose safe.

4. Fold each side of the plane so that the folded corners meet at the center crease.

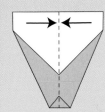

5. Next fold the plane along the center crease.

6. Open the wings.

7. Launch your plane and watch it fly!

Reread your instructions to make sure that you have included all of the steps.

Using a Sequence Chart to Instruct

A sequence chart is a **graphic organizer**. It tells the steps of an event or a process. A sequence chart can be a good way to give instructions. A sequence chart can also be a way for you to organize the information you want to include in your instructions. You may want to tell someone how to plant and care for a bean plant. Each step in the process is placed in a box. The boxes are arranged in order. The first step in the process is written in the first box, the second step is written in the second box, and so on. As always, each part of your instructions should be clear and easy to follow.

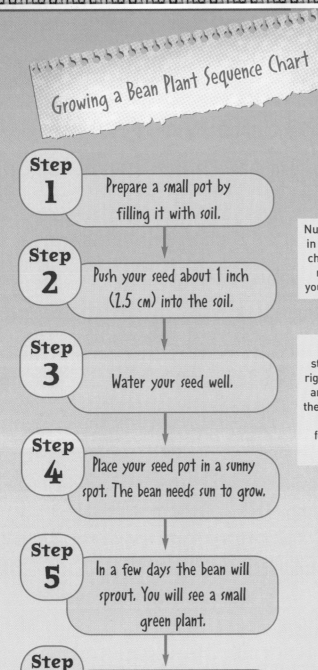

Growing a Bean Plant Sequence Chart

Step 1 Prepare a small pot by filling it with soil.

Step 2 Push your seed about 1 inch (2.5 cm) into the soil.

Step 3 Water your seed well.

Step 4 Place your seed pot in a sunny spot. The bean needs sun to grow.

Step 5 In a few days the bean will sprout. You will see a small green plant.

Step 6 Water your plant once a week, so the soil stays moist.

Number the steps in your sequence chart to help the reader follow your instructions.

Be sure your steps are in the right order. If they are out of order the reader will not succeed in following your directions!

Science Experiments

To prove that something is scientifically **accurate**, scientists perform an experiment many times. They write down the results and compare them with the results of other experiments. Students can follow instructions written by scientists to re-create the experiment and the results. In your science class, you may be asked to write the steps of an experiment to prove a scientific **fact**. To do this, first, state the science fact that you would like to prove. Make a list of the materials and equipment that you will need to do the experiment. Next, describe the process in steps. Finally, give the results.

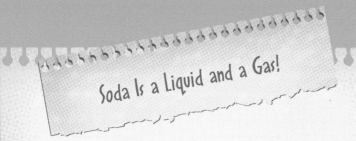

Soda Is a Liquid and a Gas!

Scientific Fact:

Soda is a solution, or mixture, of a liquid, such as water, and a gas, such as air. When you open a can or a bottle of soda, the hiss you hear is the sound of escaping gas.

State the scientific fact to be proved.

Materials:

One pitcher, 2 cups (473 ml) water, 2 tablespoons (30 ml) powdered sugar, 3 tablespoons (44 ml) baking soda, 2 tablespoons (30 ml) lemon juice, and food coloring.

Write instructions for the materials used.

Procedure:

1. Pour the water into the pitcher.
2. Add the powdered sugar and a few drops of food coloring.
3. Stir in the baking soda and lemon juice.
4. Stir well, then drink and enjoy your soda!

Describe the procedure, which is the instructions for the steps the reader must follow.

Results:

The bubbles you see and hear are bubbles of carbon dioxide, a kind of gas, that are escaping from the mixture.

Write what the results of your experiment should be, so that the reader will know whether he or she followed the instructions correctly.

Instructions for a Recipe

Recipes are lists of ingredients, or the things you need to make the recipe, and step-by-step instructions for cooking. To share a favorite recipe with a friend, make sure that you list the ingredients in the order in which they are used. Write the correct measurement, or amount, needed for each ingredient. Describe how to prepare the ingredients. Write how long your dish will take to cook, what it will look like when it is cooked, and how to serve it.

Write Right!

Some recipes suggest adding an ingredient "to taste," rather than an amount. This means the cook can add as much or as little as he or she wants.

Toaster-Oven Pizza

Makes:

6 servings

Preparation time:

About 15 minutes

Equipment:

One toaster oven, 1 fork, 1 spoon, 1 sheet of aluminum foil.

Ingredients:

Six English muffins, 1 jar of tomato or pizza sauce, 8 ounces (227 mg) mozzarella cheese, and 1 small container of Parmesan cheese.

Preparation:

Separate the English muffin halves with a fork. Toast them in the toaster oven until lightly browned. Remove the muffin halves and place them on aluminum foil. Spread tomato sauce or pizza sauce on each half. Sprinkle with the mozzarella cheese and Parmesan cheese. Return muffin halves to the toaster. Broil, or cook, until the cheese is bubbly.

Enjoy!

If you are writing a recipe, be sure that your directions are clear and well-organized.

If you must use a stove or an oven, always have an adult help you.

Gather all of your ingredients before you start to make the recipe.

Using Maps as Resources

Maps are small drawings of large places. They give people instructions on how to find their way across town, across the country, or across the world. Most maps have a **compass rose**. A compass rose is a small drawing that points to the directions north, south, east, and west on the map. Maps also have **symbols** of objects and places, such as mountains, rivers, streets, highways, and buildings. A map has a scale that compares the size of an area on the map with the real area on Earth. Maps have many other elements. Take a look in an **atlas** that is written for students and find your way around the world.

Making a Map

Create a map of your neighborhood to give someone instructions for finding his or her way from your house to your school or to another location. Draw a symbol of your house and label it "My House." Next draw the roads between your house and your school and label them. Draw a symbol of the school building and label it "My School." You can add symbols for other places and objects, such as a ballpark, a grocery store, trees, and a lake, and label them.

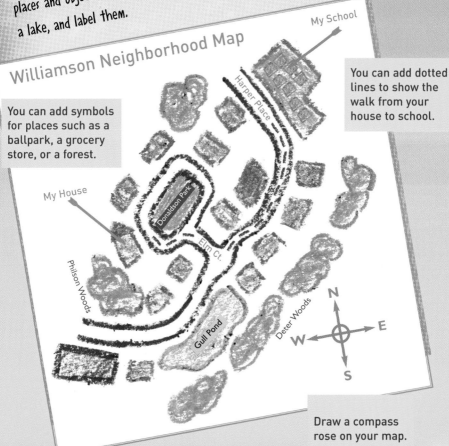

Williamson Neighborhood Map

My School

You can add dotted lines to show the walk from your house to school.

You can add symbols for places such as a ballpark, a grocery store, or a forest.

My House

Harper Place

Donaldson Park

Elm Ct.

Philson Woods

Gull Pond

Deter Woods

N
W — E
S

Draw a compass rose on your map.

Writing a Speech That Instructs

Do you have to make a speech in class this year? Here is how to write and present a speech that instructs. Choose a subject you know well. Organize your speech by writing the information in an outline. Next write each idea or fact that you will discuss on a 3-by-5-inch (8-by-13-cm) card. Arrange the cards in the order in which you will use them. Then practice your speech. Present your speech to members of your family. Are your instructions clear? Is the speech too long or too short? When you give your speech, speak clearly. Look at your cards, if you need to. Look at the faces in your **audience** and remember to smile!

Choose a subject that you feel comfortable talking about. As always, make sure your instructions are clear and easy to follow.

Time your speech before you give it to an audience to see if it is too long or too short.

How to Adopt a Dog
By Alicia Brewster

Adopting a dog from the American Society for the Prevention of Cruelty to Animals (ASPCA) is one of the best things my family ever did. Here is how to do it. Visit the ASPCA. There are many dogs and cats that need homes there. Your parents must first fill out a form promising to take care of the dog or the cat. A counselor brings out dogs or cats for you and your family to meet. A week later, someone from the ASPCA visits your home to see if your family would be good pet owners. Then you go back to the ASPCA to pick a dog or a cat. We chose Bingo, a two-year-old dog. She looks like a wolf, and she is very sweet. She was a little scared and confused at first, but after a few weeks she loved to cuddle with me whenever I sat down. Dad says Bingo is his dog. Maybe that is because she brings him the newspaper after dinner. Bingo and I know that she is really my dog!

Helpful Words That Instruct

Include strong action words to help make your instructions clear. For example, you might tell your reader to "shake" the powder and water to make lemonade rather than saying "mix." Use words between steps, such as "first," "now," "next," and "then," to give your instructions a sense of order. Improve your writing to instruct by using words that describe colors, sizes, amounts, and times. Details such as "stir the mixture slowly for five minutes," or "enter through the bright blue door," will help the reader to succeed in following your instructions.

Glossary

accurate (A-kyuh-rit) Exactly right.

assemble (uh-SEM-bul) To put something together.

atlas (AT-les) A book of maps.

audience (AH-dee-ints) A group of people who watch or listen to something.

compass rose (KUM-pus ROHZ) A drawing on a map that shows directions.

details (DEE-taylz) Extra facts.

equipment (uh-KWIP-mint) All the supplies needed to do an activity.

fact (FAKT) Something known to be real or true.

graphic organizer (GRA-fik OR-guh-ny-zer) Charts, graphs, and pictures that sort facts and ideas and make them clear.

information (in-fer-MAY-shun) Knowledge or facts.

instruct (in-STRUKT) To give explanations or directions.

instructions (in-STRUK-shunz) Explanations or directions.

introductory paragraph (in-truh-DUK-tuh-ree PAR-uh-graf) A group of sentences at the beginning of a written account that explains what is going to follow.

materials (muh-TEER-ee-ulz) What things are made of.

symbols (SIM-bulz) Objects or pictures that stand for something else.

Index

Web Sites

Due to the changing nature of Internet links, PowerKids Press has developed an online list of Web sites related to the subject of this book. This site is updated regularly. Please use this link to access the list:
www.powerkidslinks.com/wnkw/writinst/